Buster

Denise Fleming

For Warfy–the best dog ever
(1983–2001)

This edition is published by special arrangement with Henry Holt and Company, LLC.

Grateful acknowledgment is made to Henry Holt and Company, LLC for permission to reprint *Buster* by Denise Fleming. Copyright © 2003 by Denise Fleming.

Printed in China

ISBN 10   0-15-356572-1
ISBN 13   978-0-15-356572-4

The illustrations were created by pouring colored cotton fiber through hand-cut stencils.
Book design by Denise Fleming and David Powers. Visit www.denisefleming.com.

BUSTER

Buster was a happy dog.

He had everything he could ever want.

He had dishes with his name
painted on them in curvy letters,

ster

a large grassy yard

with a tall oak tree to nap under,

a sandpit for taking dirt baths,

an in-and-out flap
on the back door,

a basketful of toys,

a radio tuned to his
favorite station,

and Brown Shoes, who
took Buster to the park
whenever Buster asked.

Buster was a happy dog until Brown Shoes brought home the big box.

THE BIG BOX

Buster stared at the big box.

He hoped there were juicy steaks or fancy French cheeses
or spicy sausages in the big box.

But there were no steaks, no cheeses,
no sausages in the box.
There was just a bag of sand,
a large flat pan, two small dishes,
and a cat named Betty.
Buster was not happy.
Buster was afraid of cats.

BETTY

Betty jumped down off the table.
She began to purr and twist and
turn around Buster's legs.

Buster was terrified.

He was afraid to move.

"If I ignore her," thought Buster,

"maybe she'll go away."

Betty did everything to attract Buster's attention.
She slept in Buster's dishes with the curvy letters.
Buster ignored her.

She ran up and down and around Buster's tree.
Buster ignored her.

She dug in Buster's sandpit.
Buster ignored her.

She ran in and out and in and out the in-and-out flap.

Buster ignored her.

She hid Buster's toys.

Buster ignored her.

Then she changed the station on Buster's radio. That was *too* much for Buster.

A FINE PARK

Buster slipped under the fence.

He ran down the block,
over five streets,

and around two corners
until he came to a park.

Not his usual park but a fine park with tall trees,
a bubbling fountain, tubs of flowers, large grassy patches,
and not a cat in sight.

"No Betty," thought Buster
as he drank from the fountain.

"No Betty," thought Buster
as he rolled in the sand.

"No Betty," thought Buster as he listened to his favorite radio station.

"No Betty," thought Buster as he fell asleep in the shade of a tall tree.

LOST

Buster woke up.

He was hungry.

He was lonely.

Soon it would be dark.

Buster was ready to go home.

He looked up the street.

He looked down the street.

Nothing looked familiar.

Buster circled the park to the left.

He circled the park to the right.

Buster had no idea which direction was home. Buster was lost.

Buster asked the big yellow dog if he knew which way was home.

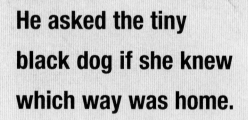

He asked the tiny black dog if she knew which way was home.

He asked the man sweeping the walks if he
knew which way was home.

No one in the park had any idea where
Buster lived.

Buster sat very still and tried to remember
the route he'd taken to the park.

But he'd been so busy trying to get away
from Betty that he hadn't paid any attention.

HOME

All Buster could think about was how he would never see his home, his dishes, his sandpit, his toys, his tree, or Brown Shoes again.

What would he do?

Where would he go?

Just then a pigeon circled Buster.

It landed close to Buster's ear.

"Coo ca coooo," said the pigeon, looking up.

Buster looked up, way up.

In the top of a tall tree several streets over,

Buster saw a waving ball of white fur.

The tree looked very familiar.

The waving ball of fur looked very familiar.

It was Betty!

Buster ran out of the park,
around two corners,
over five streets,
turned left,
and ran up the block,
all the time keeping an eye on Betty.

Buster

Park

A Fine

Campbell Circle

Indigo Drive

Martha Drive

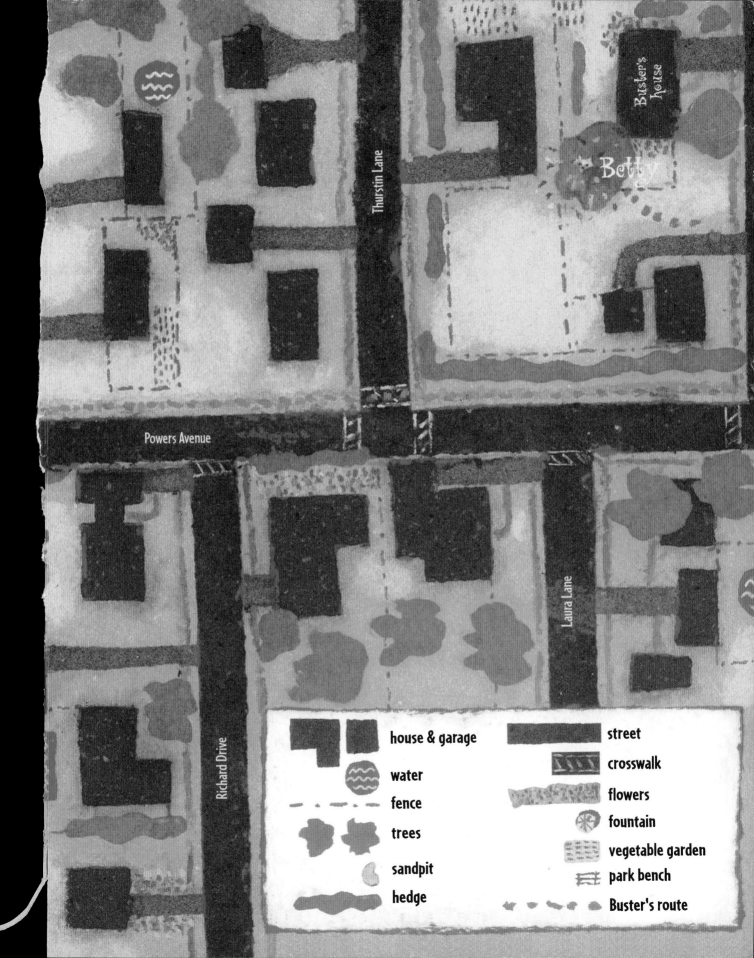

Buster's house

Betty

Thirstin Lane

Laura Lane

Powers Avenue

Richard Drive

house & garage

water

fence

trees

sandpit

hedge

street

crosswalk

flowers

fountain

vegetable garden

park bench

Buster's route

Buster slipped under the fence.

Betty ran down the tree and over to Buster.

Betty began to purr and twist and turn around Buster's legs.
Buster was a happy dog.

He had everything he could ever want—
and **more**.